Teaching
Memoir Writing

20 Easy Mini-Lessons and
Thought-Provoking Activities That Inspire Kids
to Reflect on and Write about Their Lives

BY PERDITA FINN

SCHOLASTIC
PROFESSIONAL BOOKS

NEW YORK • TORONTO • LONDON • AUCKLAND • SYDNEY
MEXICO CITY • NEW DELHI • HONG KONG

Acknowledgments

Fourteen years ago I casually attended Lucy Calkins' Summer Institute on the Teaching of Writing. At the end of two weeks, I found the love of writing I had lost in high school, and I realized that I wanted to be a teacher. I cannot thank Lucy enough for her inspiration and guidance.

I must also thank Marge Boyle, my writing teacher that summer and years later, by a happy coincidence, my colleague and friend. She was especially helpful with an earlier version of this book.

I have been lucky in the teachers I have had the opportunity to work with, and I thank particularly Julie Housum, Ghislaine Tulou, Fran Prolman, Alex Newmark, Susan Elliott, Bill Stroud, and the dedicated staff of the Urban Peace Academy.

At home, I thank my children, Sophie and Jonah, not only for their patience, but for their insistence that I tell them yet another and another story from when I was a little girl. Each day they remind me of the importance of memory. I thank my husband Clark for everything—computer lessons, proofreading, childcare, and continual encouragement.

Finally, I must acknowledge the many students I have taught over the years. I have learned from their struggles and their dedication. More than anyone, they have taught me how to write and how to teach.

"War" from KNOTS IN MY YO-YO STRING by Jerry Spinelli Copyright © 1998 by Jerry Spinelli. Reprinted by permission of Alfred A. Knopf, Inc.

"My Name" from THE HOUSE ON MANGO STREET. Copyright © 1984 by Sandra Cisneros. Published by Vintage Books, a division of Random House, Inc. and in hardcover by Alfred A. Knopf in 1994. Reprinted by permission of Susan Bergholz Literary Services, New York. All rights reserved.

Cover design by Kelli Thompson
Interior design by Kathy Massaro
Interior photographs on pages 4, 7, 11, 13, 14, 33, and 52 by Oi Pin Chan; page 8: NASA.

ISBN 0-439-04390-5

Contents

Introduction

Writing is an act of thinking. Its primary purpose is to find meaning, a meaning so powerful that it should be shared through writing.

—Donald Murray

Like most teachers, when I first started to teach writing, I accepted the common wisdom that my students' work would be good if they wrote about what they knew—their interests and concerns, their struggles and triumphs. When students write from their own experience, their work can have authority and specificity. But those first years, I must admit, I had to wade through a lot of tedious accounts of video games, slumber parties, and trips to the mall.

I did mini-lessons on adding specific details, playing with leads, and experimenting with dialogue, but for the most part the same pieces just got longer. My students could fill up their notebooks with freewriting and carve out stories and personal narratives, but with few exceptions they were approaching their writing as stenographers instead of artists. How could I get them to explore the meaning of what they were writing about and let their writing take them on a journey of discovery?

I began to have my students play with critical- and creative-thinking exercises. We practiced generating questions, making connections, and generating metaphors. We experimented with juxtaposition and point of view. How many different ways can we look at the same thing? I asked them. What happens when we connect stories? What kinds of new meanings begin to emerge?

The writing in my classroom changed—it became thoughtful, artistic, more interesting to read. My students began to look at the experiences of their lives as material they could play with in the creation of a work of art rather than an event they had an obligation to record with complete fidelity. Their writing became significant. And they weren't writing personal narratives anymore, I realized. They were writing memoirs.

What is Memoir?

Sometimes when I tell people how much I love writing memoir with my students, they look confused and laugh, "But how can ten- or twelve-year-olds reminisce about the good ol' days, fondly recall long-gone friends, and set their lives in order?"

Many people think of memoir as something written at the end of a life. In fact it is really just the exploration of a memory, sometimes many memories. The questions that concern the memoir writer—who am I, and what has made me who I am?—can be asked at any point in one's life. We can as easily look at what happened to us yesterday as we can look at what happened ten years ago or even before we were born.

On the verge of their new identity as teenagers, preadolescents are eager to collect and examine their memories and to use those memories to make sense of where they find themselves now. Twelve-year-old Jessica wrote a story about how she fell out of a tree and then connected it with the stories her mother had told her of how she always used to fall out of her bed when she was a little girl. "And now," says Jessica, "I keep falling in love."

In an earlier writing workshop, Jessica might just have written a flat account of falling out of a tree and breaking her leg, but when she wrote "Falling" in my class on memoir, she noticed a subtle and important pattern in her life and was able to create a vivid, fresh piece of writing from those realizations. At its best, writing is an exploration of our own hearts and minds. As we write, we discover what we think, what we know, what we care about, who we are.

Memoir is an increasingly popular genre. Annie Dillard, the author of *An American Childhood*, attributes its appeal to its lack of conventional rules. Not confined to straightforward narrative, it can combine history, science, philosophy, poetry, and even fiction, as does Dillard's account of coming of age in Pittsburgh in the fifties. It is a genre in which all other genres can mingle and redefine themselves. Yet, while the possibilities for experimentation are definitely exciting, I think the real reason for memoir's current success has more to do with the implicit assertion of memoir that every life matters. For while autobiography is usually about famous people and the big, public events that have made them so celebrated, memoir is often about very ordinary folk and the transformative moments of their ordinary lives.

After a recent vacation, my five-year-old daughter and I sat down with our photos, a box of crayons, and a lot of paper to create a memory book. My idea was to record the events from each day—the whale watch, the trip to see the dunes, the big sand castle we all made at the beach—but my daughter had a different plan.

Sophie drew a picture of herself and her beloved cousin Adam turning on the outdoor shower and making an enormous puddle, and then one of them picking all the blue blossoms off the hydrangea. Finally, she spent a long time depicting the two of them rifling through her father's suitcase and putting on all of his boxer shorts. "Me and Adam had a lot of fun getting into trouble this vacation," she giggled.

I had not invested the project with much meaning other than recording our vacation. My daughter, on the other hand, had organized her significant moments from the trip around a theme. She had created a memoir, and as I looked at her pictures later that night I found myself wondering what had been important to *me* about the trip.

I realized that my own memoir would be about the ocean that I missed now that I lived far away in the mountains. It would be about low tide, about a cloudy day with white caps in the distance, about the red seaweed that gets caught in my hair, about my grandmother who swam in that ocean every day of the year until she died.

Memoir in the Classroom

Writing memoir is not just about recording what happened to us, but about exploring the possible significance of an event or important moment. How do we decide what is important enough to write about? How do we discover what is not so ordinary about our ordinary lives?

Over the years I have collected and created various exercises to help my students deepen their thinking and broaden their vision. The first mini-lessons in this book will help students access various significant moments from their lives. They will begin to look more closely at their inner and outer worlds. There is some thought that all our memories exist within us. How de we tap into them? How do we rediscover them?

The next set of mini-lessons is designed to help students explore the meanings of these memories. Using a number of critical- and creative-thinking exercises, students will explore their memoirs as metaphors, recognize connections, and search for themes. They will then begin taking all the fragments they have written and set about shaping a complete piece of writing—learning how to let go of their allegiance to recording the event and to begin focusing on the techniques of telling a story instead.

When I teach memoir to my students—usually after they have developed a certain amount of fluency in writing in their notebooks—I begin by reading many different kinds of memoir with them. We read lots of picture books, excerpts from chapter books, and current magazine essays. I set up literature groups where each group picks a longer memoir to read and study together.

The best way to learn a language is to go to a country where it is spoken and immerse yourself in listening, reading, talking, and writing it. The best way to learn about the possibilities and expectations for a particular genre of writing is to spend as much time with it as you can.

I usually allow six to eight weeks for a genre study so that students can have a thorough experience of each phase of the writing process. I move through the mini-lessons sequentially, allowing days for the literature groups to meet and discuss their reading and for the whole class to discuss certain shorter pieces that I have included here.

I have also used the activities in this book to supplement other reading and writing projects, and have adapted the curriculum when doing interdisciplinary classes with other teachers. Memoir does not need to be taught exclusively in a writing workshop but can be successfully integrated into many other related areas of study.

Memoir and Science

Some of the most wonderful memoirs have been written by scientists who have wanted to explore how they awoke to the natural world. As a child, the zoologist Gerald Durrell spent hours watching insects and small animals and has written hilarious accounts of his observations. Diane Ackerman and Annie Dillard have examined closely their sensory perceptions and personal histories, and one of the most famous memoirs of all—Thoreau's *Walden*—is a profound exploration of how one man discovered his meaning in nature.

Memoir is not just writing about what happened to us or what we did. It is also about what we have noticed, heard, felt, and tasted. I once worked with a science teacher who was doing a unit on animals. We began by having the students write extensively about their own experiences with pets and creatures they had watched in the wild. We taught them to look carefully at what they remembered. What did they already know that they weren't aware of knowing?

Another time, when the same teacher was doing a unit on the water cycle, we had the students explore their memories of water. One student wrote about Manhattan's East River and how she tried at sunset each day to find a way to watch the colors changing on the water. Where did that water come from? asked the teacher. Where was it going?

Sometimes our own bodies can inspire research. Oliver Sacks, the famous neurologist, broke his leg very badly as a young man and experienced an unsettling disassociation from his body. What was happening in his brain, and why? Later Sacks wrote *A Leg to Stand On*, a very entertaining memoir about what he had experienced and later researched about his condition.

Much of science is about careful observation and questioning. It is just these skills that students are practicing when they compose memoir.

Memoir and Social Studies

Some of us have experienced the pleasure of looking at the front page of a newspaper from the day we were born—at the headlines, at what was happening in the public realm when we were entering the world so privately. What is our connection to those events? There was a show on television a few years ago, *The Wonder Years*, that was structured as a memoir. An older man recalled his very ordinary childhood travails against the backdrop of the Vietnam War and the turbulent social changes of the sixties. The boy barely noticed what was happening around him, but the man realized just how much those larger events had affected his day-to-day experience as a child.

Sometimes I have had students research what was happening in the wider world around them at the time of the episodes they are writing about. The discoveries can be profound. A student who was writing about her first experience of racism when she was eight years old discovered that the riots in Crown Heights were erupting at the very same time. She hadn't known about those events in far-off New York City, but when she learned of them later, each event illuminated the other. The personal was part of a wider societal pattern. The historical became immediate and intimately felt.

In our own country's history, memoir has had a significant place. From Benjamin Franklin and Walt Whitman to James Baldwin and Maxine Hong Kingston, our writers have explored not just who they are, but what it means to be an American. When I team-taught United States History, I had my eighth graders address the question of how this country was shaping them and how they would shape it. We asked them to reflect, from a very personal place, on what it meant to be an American.

Memoir and Art

One year I was lucky enough to have an artist-in-residence who came regularly to work with my writing workshop. We were studying memoir at the time, and John was fascinated by the kinds of questions we were asking. He began by sharing with the kids many different kinds of self-portraits artists had done—from Rembrandt and Van Gogh to Picasso's abstractions. He talked with the class about the language of painting, about color and texture, light and shadow, and eventually the students did their own self-portraits to go along with the memoirs they were writing. Their explorations in each medium enhanced their understanding of the other.

More simply, I have often had students illustrate their memoirs and create their own picture books from them. For many students (and writers too!) drawing is a way into writing—a picture will lead them to a story or the revision of a story—and as they attend to the details of their artwork, they frequently become more aware of the language they are using. Some of the most wonderful memoirs have been created by artists who were both writers and illustrators—Robert McCloskey, Patricia Polacco, Donald Crews, Tomie de Paola.... The list goes on and on (see the bibliography on pages 62–64). One of the most powerful recent memoirs is Art Spiegelman's *Maus*, an account of his parents' experiences in the Holocaust, presented with chilling irony in the style of a comic book.

No matter how they are eventually used, all of the various mini-lessons are designed to help students discover meaning inside of them. When we write more, we see more. Not only does our writing get better as we learn to look more creatively at the world around us; the way we look at our lives begins to change as well. My students' writing got better when we started writing memoir together, but something even more important happened. The way my students thought about things shifted—they noticed more, wondered more. Their writing became for them a vital part of being alive.

The Workshop Classroom— Routines and Rituals

That writing is a process that involves prewriting, drafting, and revision is readily accepted these days, and many teachers—including Donald Graves, Lucy Calkins, and Nancy Atwell—have shared with us their strategies for structuring their writing workshop classrooms. The struggle for me as a teacher has always been how to provide my students with adequate time for experimenting with their writing while keeping the energy of the classroom moving forward. How do I create realistic yet challenging expectations? As a writer, I know I need time just to scribble junk in my notebook in order to figure out what I really want to say. But I also know how much it motivates me to have signed a contract and to have to produce a piece of writing.

The exercises and activities in this book are designed to help students make the most of each phase of the writing process. In addition, I have explained certain routines from my own classroom that reinforce lessons and help my students develop a disciplined practice with their writing.

1 Mini-Lessons

At the beginning of class each day, I engage my students in an activity that will help them explore some aspect of the writing process, or of the genre we are studying together. After the activity, I usually provide them with less structured time for writing in their notebooks and talking about writing so they can discover to what new places the work we've just done may take them. Some students may even want to try the activity again or go back to one from the day before. If the activity has taken the whole period, I will usually schedule more writing time for the next day.

With each mini-lesson in this book, I have offered both an explanation of the purpose of the exercise and an activity to help clarify and practice it. In some cases, I also have provided alternative ways of doing a mini-lesson or of connecting it with another subject.

2 Writing and Conferencing

Young writers need time to write, and it is while they are actually writing in class that I find I can teach them the most. It's a time to help those who are stuck, to make others aware of what they may unknowingly have discovered about writing, to prod, to refine, to clarify, and to reassure.

I try to remember that I am teaching the writer and not the piece of writing, and I therefore keep both criticism of and applause for the work to a minimum. When a student asks me if her or his work is any good, I often smile and counter, "Is it?" I want them to develop their own standards and confidence.

3 Reading and Writing Connections

In order to help my students learn how to talk about their own and their peers' writing, I make time each week to read and discuss a work in the genre that we are currently studying. I have worked hard to train my students in discussion techniques that provide them with the skills for cooperatively exploring a text instead of depending on me for answers. I want them to learn to talk as writers about a piece of writing.

In this book I have included two memoirs (pages 56–61) which exemplify many of the different points of the mini-lessons. They are also richly layered and sure to provoke interesting classroom discussions.

In addition to our class readings, I also have students study a longer memoir in their literature groups. Suggestions for appropriate texts are listed in the bibliography (pages 62–64).

4 Writing Groups

Every night after a day of writing, my husband and I sit down together eager to share whatever we have come up with that day—whether it's a paragraph, a whole chapter, or just a new way of thinking about an issue we're writing about. We talk and talk, and in that talking we often discover new ways of saying what we want to say, or we figure out what we want to write about tomorrow.

It's important to bring our writing to a supportive audience *while we are working on it* and not just after it is finished. The literature groups in my classroom are also students' writing groups during the genre study. They share their work at the end of each day, help each other come up with ideas and choose pieces to revise, and finally work cooperatively with each other on copyediting and proofreading.

Collecting Material

Starting a Writer's Notebook

One of the habits of creative people is that they generate enormous amounts of raw material—painters do hundreds of doodles and sketches, inventors try experiment after experiment, and writers fill notebook after notebook with scattered thoughts, bits and pieces of description, ramblings, observations, snatches of dialogue, whole stories, and single words. In order to come up with a single great idea, we need to come up with a lot of lesser ideas.

A movie I saw years ago, about the sculptress Camille Claudel, opened with her roaming the streets of Paris in the middle of the night with her wheelbarrow. She dug in the parks, in people's backyards, in graveyards, slowly accumulating masses of wet dark clay that she pushed home just at dawn and dumped on her studio floor. As the first rays of light seeped into her room, she extracted a large lump, pulled out the pebbles and grit, and began to sculpt.

When we begin the writing process, we need to collect our clay. We need to gather it from a lot of different places because clay from different sources has different qualities and uses and, most of all, we need to collect a lot of it.

I have two expectations for my students' notebooks:

1. quantity of material   2. variety of material

Quantity

Natalie Goldberg, the author of *Writing Down the Bones*, began a workshop I did with her by saying, "I give you permission to write the worst junk in the world." Wow!

It's amazing how much easier it is to come up with words and sentences when you are no longer worried if they are good or right or smart. The paradox, of course, is that once you stop striving for excellence, your writing usually relaxes and becomes more natural. Often, it gets better as well. Toni Morrison says that she never minds writing badly, as she knows that whenever she wants she can go back and change it.

I have certain rules for myself that I share with my students to help them become more fluent as writers:

1. Don't think—just write.

Writing *is* thinking. As soon as we begin to write, the images and ideas begin pouring onto the page. One thought leads to another. If we sit at our desks staring into space and waiting for inspiration, it usually doesn't come.

I frequently give my students (and myself) timed writings where we are expected to write without stopping for ten or fifteen minutes. Like any physical exercise, the more regularly we do this, the easier it becomes.

2. Spelling, handwriting, grammar, and punctuation don't matter (for now).

What matters is the flow of words, that I capture the thoughts the moment they emerge in my imagination. Anything that stops that flow—asking how to spell a word, worrying about whether or not to use a comma, making artistic flourishes with our letters—is not important at this point.

Of course, it's okay to spell a word correctly or use punctuation well, it's just not something to be concerned about. It is often necessary for me to remind students, however, that while I am not looking for perfect handwriting, their writing will be useless to them if it's completely illegible.

3. Carry your notebook with you at all times.

Once you begin working on a project—writing a memoir, for instance—the ideas do not arrive on a regularly scheduled basis. Ideas can come to us at anytime, anywhere, and unless you scribble them in your notebook right then and there, you are apt to lose them. I keep a notebook right next to the shower in the morning and a small one in my back pocket when I am hiking, and I frequently tape into my notebook restaurant napkins with sentences scrawled across them.

I play games with my students, checking up on them in the hallway, in the cafeteria, in science class, to make sure they have their notebooks with them, and most of all I read the notebooks frequently to see that they are working on their writing outside of class.

Variety

When I ask for variety from my students, I am not just asking that they try out different topics but also different ways of writing—dialogue, descriptions, dreams, shifts in point of view. The notebook is where we rehearse and play, where we can try out anything, put on any costume we want. It doesn't matter if our experiments are successes or failures—for now it matters only that we try.

Frequently, students need encouragement so they don't get stuck just writing love poems or complaints or accounts of the day. The notebook is not a diary after all. I provide students with a list of the kinds of writing I expect to see in their notebooks. Such a list might include:

conversations	explanations	memories
descriptions	thinking out loud	imaginings
jottings	thoughts	guesses
quick notes	ideas	wrong answers
word lists	wonderings	possibilities
dreams	questions	letters
observations	plays	poems
announcements	stories	interesting information

The notebook is a record of anything and everything that passes through the writer's mind. The objective is to collect it all and not discard anything. For when one is working on a piece, it is very difficult to know beforehand what is useful. Some writing that seems digressive or inconsequential may actually lead us to a crucial thought. Most writers will say that when they are working on a piece they are working on it all the time—whether they are conscious of it or not. Later, students will reread their notebooks and decide what is useful, but for now the challenge is just to collect everything, as much clay as they can.

MINI-LESSON

Who am I?
What has made me who I am?

There was a child went forth every day,
And the first object he looked upon and received with
wonder or pity or love or dread, that object he became,
And that object became part of him for the day or a certain
part of the day . . . or for many years or stretching
cycles of years.

The early lilacs became part of this child,
And grass, and white and red morning-glories, and white and
red clover, and the song of the phoebe-bird,
And the March-born lambs, and the sow's pink-faint litter,
and the mare's foal, and the cow's calf, and the noisy
brood of the barnyard or by the mire of the pond-side
. . . and the fish suspending themselves so curiously
below there . . . and the beautiful curious liquid . . . and
the water-plants with their graceful flat heads . . . all
became part of him.

from "There Was A Child Went Forth,"
by Walt Whitman

Everything we have seen and touched and heard and experienced has, in some way, made us who we are. Whitman considers all the many things in just one day that will touch on the life of a child. From here he goes on to think about the child's teachers and classmates, the people he passes on his way to school, his parents, the streets he walks, and finally the changing light of sunset, and a solitary bird flying across the sky.

Who am I? Activity

You may want to share the whole poem with your class or just the excerpt above. Either way it serves as an invitation to your students to think about all the many things that have (either obviously or subtly) affected them in their own lives.

   Using the activity worksheet sheet provided, have students begin to make their own lists of influences that they can write about later. Of course, there is room on the sheet for students to create their own categories, and they may want to share these with each other.

After creating their lists, have the students choose just one of the items to write about in their notebooks. At various times throughout the genre study, students may want to return to these lists, either to add to them or to use them for inspiration in their writing.

Themes and Variations

A list could also be created simply by noting all the details of a single day, as does Whitman in his poem. Have students carry their notebooks with them, jotting down all that crosses their path from morning to night. What do they notice? What's important to them?

WORKSHEET

Who am I? What has made me who I am?

People

Relatives	Friends	Teachers	Other
Mom	Cal	Ms Clare	
Dad	Noah		
Pop-pop			
Ralph			

Places

Homes	Special Places	Vacations	Travel Routes
Our home now – the only place I've ever lived.	The Park	The Beach	

Nature

Trees and Plants	Weather	Water	Other
I have a favorite tree in the park. Everyone likes to climb it.	I hate thunderstorms. I love snow.	I like any kind of water because I love to swim	

Stories

Books	Television	Movies	Family Stories
Harry Potter! Star Wars books	The Simpsons	Star Wars	

19

WORKSHEET

Who am I? What has made me who I am?

Animals

Pets	Wild Animals	Insects	Other
Sasha— our dog		I hate bugs— especially spiders!	
My lizard			

Sensations

Food	Smells	Music	Other
apples ice cream Chocolate	cinnamon apple pie	I like Will Smith a lot!	

Diversions

Games	Sports	Dreams	Daydreams
Zelda	Baseball Soccer Swimming	Design a video game	

20

Who am I? What has made me who I am?

People

Relatives	Friends	Teachers	Other

Places

Homes	Special Places	Vacations	Travel Routes

Nature

Trees and Plants	Weather	Water	Other

Stories

Books	Television	Movies	Family Stories

Who am I? What has made me who I am?

Animals

Pets   Wild Animals   Insects   Other

Sensations

Food   Smells   Music   Other

Diversions

Games   Sports   Dreams   Daydreams

MINI·LESSON 2

Timelines and Stepping-Stones

Transitions, realizations, transformations—these experiences of change are often the most meaningful and memorable to us. Sometimes they happen *to* us—we move, our parents get divorced, we meet an important friend—and sometimes they happen within our hearts—we fall in love, we realize something about our world, we understand why something happened to us.

The Timelines and Stepping-Stones Activity

First, have students create timelines of the important *events* of their lives. You may want to talk first about what kinds of events belong on a timeline—moves, starting school, triumphs, changes. Sometimes, however, I find that students are more creative about the kinds of experiences they put on their timelines if I don't talk about it too much initially. Only if the whole class is having a lot of trouble will I share with them a sample like the following.

Sample Timeline and Stepping Stones:

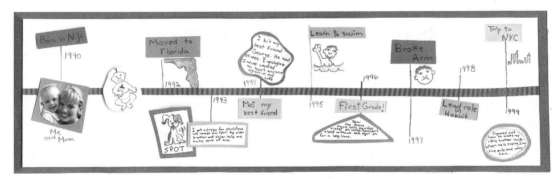

Next, have students think about the important *moments* in their lives. For instance, on my timeline I would probably have noted my parents' divorce, whereas for my stepping-stones I might have included the time I heard my parents' fighting and realized how badly they were getting along. The timeline records the public event, the stepping-stone the private moment.

Themes and Variations

Instead of thinking about the stepping-stones along the path of an entire life, it is possible to focus on a single period of life, a relationship, or even one experience, and think about what moments from it stand out. This can be an excellent way of looking more closely at something that has happened to us.

MINI·LESSON 3

Emotions versus Details— Writing about What Happened

My grandpa wears soft shirts and tan sandals with socks.
Nothing scratches me when I hug him.

from *Grandpa*, by Barbara Borack

"I was so happy when…" or "I was so angry that…"

Times of extreme emotion are very compelling to write about. Unfortunately, just talking about the feeling often leaves the reader uninterested. The challenge as a writer is to allow the reader to have the experience we had and thus feel the same emotion. The soft clothes and colors and sounds of Barbara Borack's description of her grandfather convey her comfortable affection for him. She doesn't *tell* us how she feels about him—she *shows* us.

Emotions versus Details Activity

Ask your students to think about a time when they were very angry or happy or sad or scared. Have them shut their eyes and visualize the moment of most extreme feeling. What do they see? What do they touch, smell, and hear? Tell them to open their eyes and write down all the details of that moment, without ever describing or naming the emotion itself.

It can be fun to have your students then share their descriptions with each other and see if they have conveyed a sense of what they were feeling. After sharing and talking with their classmates, they may want to go back to their writing and add or change some details. Students usually enjoy this exercise and want to repeat it a number of times.

Themes and Variations

For more advanced students, it can be interesting to think about how our emotions color what we see. Have them look out the window or at pictures and describe what they see. Then ask students to imagine they are very angry and describe the scenes now. What kind of language do they use? What kinds of sounds do their words have? What details do they notice?

This exercise may be repeated using different emotions—happiness, sadness, fear, and so on.

MINI-LESSON 4

Snapshots

It's so much fun to take pictures. At a birthday party, camping out in the woods, on vacation, we snap dozens and dozens. We step back to take in the whole picture, we zoom in for a close-up, we shoot the same picture from different angles. Sometimes we'll take the same picture three or four times just to make sure we capture it. Later, when the pictures are developed, we'll throw out the ones we don't like and arrange the rest in an album.

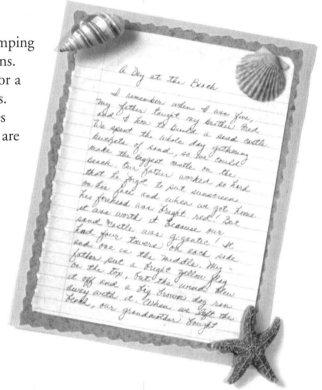

> *When I was nine we lived on a street with big trees....*
> *We lived near a railroad. Before I went to sleep, I*
> *listened to the steam locomotives. The freight trains*
> *and the express trains blew their whistles as they went*
> *racketing by in the dark. In our backyard there was*
> *a beech tree. If you climbed high enough, you could*
> *see the Hudson River and smoke from the trains.*
>
> from *When I Was Nine,*
> by James Stephenson

Snapshots Activity

In this exercise students will create an album of a particular event, or a special time (as Stephenson does) or of a particular place (as Sandra Cisneros does in *The House on Mango Street*). Instead of using photographs, however, they will make "word pictures." For example, an album about my friend Christine might begin as follows:

> *I looked over the old wooden fence and she was standing there, just my height, holding a doll, too, like mine. "My doll's named Christine," I said. "That's my name!" she smiled.*
> *All around the fence grew rhubarb, and in the early summer we'd dare each other to bite it. The green stalks were speckled with red and very sour.*
> *We ate the blackberries we found in the thick prickly bushes behind the garage, and once back there Christine stepped on a green snake in her bare feet.*

Initially, students might try to do ten pictures around a particular focus with just two or three sentences for each picture. Before they begin writing, they may want to shut their eyes for a moment and remember—sounds, smells, details. As with notebook writing, it is best to do these "word pictures" very fast without too much planning or thinking. Tell your students to remember that, as with shooting snapshots, some of the pictures don't come out, but if you take a lot of them, you'll have enough to fill your album.

MINI-LESSON

Chaining

Sometimes, in order to help us get from one image to another, it is helpful to have a refrain that we return to when we are stuck about what to write next. In his book *Wishes, Lies, and Dreams*, the poet Kenneth Koch has students make list poems beginning each line with "I wish…" or "I dream…" To help us generate material for our memoir, it may be enough to keep repeating, "I remember…" as does Paul Auster (who writes of himself in third person) in *The Invention of Solitude*:

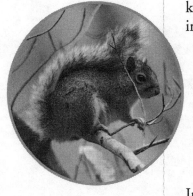

> *He remembers the sight of his father knotting his tie and saying to him, Rise and shine little boy. He remembers wanting to be a squirrel, because he wanted to be light like a squirrel and have a bushy tail and be able to jump from tree to tree as though he were flying. He remembers looking through the venetian blinds and seeing his newborn sister coming home from the hospital in his mother's arms…*

In *When I Was Young in the Mountains*, Cynthia Rylant uses the refrain of the title to take her from one image to another. My friend Julie Housum calls it "chaining" because each idea or detail is like the link in a chain, connected both to the thought in front of it and the one behind.

Chaining Activity

Using one of the starting phrases below, students will create their own memory chains, trying to collect as many details as they can. Like Paul Auster they may find they settle into one memory before going on to the next, or they may go quite rapidly from one idea to another.

Starters for Chaining:

I remember…   I used to imagine…
When we lived at…   I dreamt that…
In first grade (or second or third)…   When I was little, I used to…
In the summertime…   Every night…

Of course, students may have their own ideas for good chain starters, and they should be encouraged to use them as long as the ideas help them stay fluent in their writing.

Themes and Variations

Julie Housum used to have her students make actual paper chains on which they wrote their memories. Then she would decorate the room and surround her students with their own writing.

MINI-LESSON 6

Show and Tell

Digging around at my mother's house, I will sometimes find an old toy I have not seen in years and years. Instantly I will be flooded with memories. A smell, a piece of music, or an object—these are often the keys to unlocking much of what we thought we had forgotten about the past. In the longest and most famous memoir of all, Marcel Proust's *Remembrance of Things Past*, the taste of a madeleine, a cookie, first brings back the memory of his mother putting him to bed and then just about everything else that ever happened to Proust. In the picture book *Christmas Tree Memories*, by Aliki, the various ornaments on the Christmas tree remind the family of past fun together.

> *There is an angel I made.*
> *Remember we went to Granny's and gathered nuts and pinecones in the woods?*
> *Then we went home and baked cookies.*
> *And I made the walnut cradle.*

Show and Tell Activity

Have a day for old-fashioned show-and-tell. Each student should bring to class an object that is in some way meaningful to them. Sitting in a circle, they can take turns sharing with each other the stories behind the objects. It may be helpful as well for students to ask each other questions in order to uncover more details and background information. This activity can be done as a whole class (in which case, I've discovered, it can take a few days!) or in small groups.

After telling their stories and talking about their objects, have students write in their notebooks. They may even want to do some chaining around the objects or create another series of "word pictures."

Triggers—the Reading/Writing Connection

"That reminds me of the time… "

How often, when talking with friends, do we find ourselves remembering our own story as they tell theirs? Someone recounts how she broke her leg, and it triggers a chain of stories about other fractures, ski trips, vacations, crazy relatives. The same thing happens when we read a story—we are reminded of similar experiences in our own lives or things we've heard about from other people. Most of us, however, take little notice of these associations when we are reading and try to keep our attention on the words on the page. But writers like to talk and write, and often when they are reading, they will have pens in their hands, scribbling stories in response to what they've just read.

Triggers Activity

Read aloud a story to the class—one with a variety of different references that might be familiar to them (grandparents, a city or country story, a story about a pet). Ask the students to pay attention to what memories in their own lives are triggered by the details of the story. Explain that it might be a character, an event, or even a seemingly unimportant detail that reminds them of something. Also, the memory that's triggered might not at first seem important, but that's okay. In this early stage of collecting material, it is very hard to judge what will be useful for a later piece of writing.

I often provide students with a copy of the piece we are reading together so that they can check or underline those details that trigger memories for them. At the end of our reading, I have the students record their memories in their notebooks with as much detail as they can.

Themes and Variations

Making connections between something I am reading or learning about and something in my own life is often how I make sense of new material. I frequently have students look for points of connection in the pieces of literature we are studying together. Interestingly, it can also be a way to engage more deeply with a seemingly irrelevant history or science text. "What does this have to do with me?" students will often ask. This exercise asks them to explore that question for themselves.

MINI-LESSON 8

Inventing the Truth

Now my babushka, my grandmother, knew lots of things. She knew just how to tell a good story. She knew how to make ordinary things magical. And she knew how to make the best chocolate cake in Michigan.

After she told my brother and me a grand tale from her homeland, we'd always ask, "Bubbie, is that true?"

She'd answer, "Of course it is true, but it may not have happened!" Then she'd laugh.

from *My Rotten Redheaded Older Brother*, by Patricia Polacco

Many memoirists find ways to hint to us that they are more interested in the truth—that is, in meanings and feelings—than in what actually happened. After all, memoirists are storytellers and not reporters, and like all good storytellers, they know when to leave things out, make changes and

(Troubleshooting)

"I don't know what to write about!"

All of the mini-lessons in this section of the book are designed to help students discover a wealth of writing topics. Still, I have found that there are always one or two students who resist coming up with anything at all. Why? I think often what those students are actually saying is not, "I don't know what to write about" but "I don't want to write about my life" or "My life isn't worth writing about."

Sherenie, for instance, sat at her desk quietly each day only briefly grazing her paper with her pencil. When I tried to find out why she wasn't doing any work, she would just shrug and turn away. After a few days of this, I asked her if she would rather write something else. "Like what?" she asked. "Well, you could make up a character, a pretend person, and do all these activities as if you were her. Or you could just tell lies. Remember you're not getting graded on whether you tell the truth or not!" Sherenie smiled and the next day she began writing.

Living in a foster home and with her mother dying of AIDS, Sherenie didn't feel much like thinking about her life and sharing it with anybody else in writing. Interestingly, as soon as I allowed her the protective veil of fiction, she invented a little girl who had many of the same characteristics and experiences as herself.

Much of fiction is actually memoir in disguise. Much of memoir is actually artful invention. There are no rules about what memoir must be. As a teacher, I try to stay flexible to the needs of my students in helping them find their voices as writers.

additions, and give their imaginations free rein. When I tell the story of how my father, a surgeon, rushed our cat to the emergency room of the local hospital one night, I invent many of the details—the conversation with the switchboard operator where he told her to prep the OR because he was bringing in one of his "babies," the anxious staff waiting with a stretcher at the front door, the stitched-up cat curled up on a pillow in the recovery room. Did my father really perform surgery on our family pet? Sure he did. Is that exactly how it happened? Well….

Inventing the Truth Activity

The objective of this activity is to help students become more playful and less literal about what they remember. It begins with a game called "Two Truths and a Lie." One person tells three things about themselves, two of which are actually true and one of which is, of course, a lie. Then the players try to guess which is the lie. The person (or people) who correctly guesses the lie wins. If no one figures out the lie, then the person who lied wins. Students will discover there are many different strategies for fooling everybody—telling three outrageous things, three very ordinary details, an outrageous fact that happens to be true, and so on.

It may be fun to then read a short memoir (one of Patricia Polacco's for instance) and think about what the writer might have invented and why. Because, of course, the memoirist plays with facts for a reason—sometimes to merely entertain and sometimes to reveal a deeper truth about the story.

Now students can go to their notebooks and write one of their own memories, playing fast and loose with the literal truth. They may want to add a character to a scene, a conversation that didn't happen but could have, weather that contributes to the mood (an episode that happened in the summer might be switched to the bleak last days of autumn), or fill in all the details of something they only vaguely recall.

Students may decide to make their stories quite fantastic and include magical or fairy tale-like elements. They should be encouraged to give free rein to their imaginations with this activity.

MINI-LESSON 9

Natural Histories

Each day thousands of memories, fleeting images, and vague recollections surface briefly in our minds and disappear. What invites them into our consciousness? Why, just now, do I remember the tiled floor of my kitchen on 88th Street?

Many scientists believe that our sense of smell is the key that unlocks all the memories stored up inside of us, and I know just how powerful a reminder a scent can be—my mother's perfume, fresh-cut grass, the salty ocean air. Interestingly, Alzheimer's patients lose not only their memories but their ability to detect any odors or fragrances. But I also know that my other senses can be powerful triggers as well—I have just to hear the music of *Swan Lake*, and I am a five-year-old in love with ballet for the first time. I touch the skin, thin and translucent, of my mother's hand, and I remember holding my grandmother's hand after her stroke. And with each change of season, some barely perceptible combination of smell and sight and sound and light floods me with innumerable associations.

Natural Histories Activity

The following activities are designed to help students pay closer attention to the way their senses are triggering memories in their minds all the time.

Initially, I bring to class a variety of different items that may be evocative for the students—music from a few years earlier; some powerful scents such as perfume, paste, pencil shavings, lemon and vanilla; some seasonal items such as daffodils and pumpkins, and even some flavors—wintergreen, cherry candy. We experiment with smelling and looking and listening and tasting, and we notice what memories arise. Of course, I recognize that memory is arbitrary and idiosyncratic and that perhaps no memories or only one or two may be triggered by these items. Nevertheless, I want the students to begin to make the connection between their present sensory experiences and the act of memory.

The next day I take the students on a walk, usually just around the building, and ask them to notice the different sensations of the season—the color of the light and sky, the air, the foliage. We shut our eyes and try to notice different smells. We look around and touch the bark of a tree, the smooth metal of a railing. The students carry their notebooks with them, jotting down any memories that come up during our walk.

Finally, I give them the assignment to increase their sensory awareness

for a few days. "Listen, look, smell, taste, and touch the world around you," I say, "and see what it brings back. Keep a list in your notebooks of all the associations, and remember you don't have to have a memory of a whole story or a huge transformation but just of a moment, a gesture." Later we will explore the question of whether one of these memories led to a bigger recollection or if, in and of itself, it contained some hidden depth and meaning.

MINI-LESSON 10

Family Stories

Not only do our own experiences shape us, but the experiences of our relatives and ancestors can have a powerful influence on who we are. In *My Grandfather's Journey*, Allen Say tells about his grandfather's journey to America as a young man. His grandfather's love of California was what eventually brought the author to leave Japan. In *Miss Rumphius*, Barbara Cooney tells how her great-aunt's mission in life affected her plans for her own future. Where our ancestors came from, the stories we have been told about distant relatives we resemble, and what we imagine from the fragments of stories we have heard about distant and close family members, all have helped to create our sense of who we are and who we will be.

Interestingly, even what we don't know about our own family histories can be powerful. In *The Woman Warrior* Maxine Hong Kingston wonders if she will end up like the aunt whose name she is not even allowed to speak. She feels connected to this unnamed woman and tries to imagine what her life was like. Toni Morrison has said that, in her novels, she is trying to recover the lost memories of African American people, writing what could not be written at that time.

Family Stories Activity

We begin by sharing the stories of family members—distant and close—that we already know. Almost always there are stories of grandfathers who fought in wars, stories of famous relations, ghost stories, and stories of long-lost customs and traditions. Sometimes there are just snippets of information— "My great aunt was supposed to have been the first woman to drive a car in her neighborhood"—and sometimes whole epics: "As long as anyone can remember, the men in my family have been inventors." By telling a few stories of my own relatives, I am usually able to coax stories from my students—*if* they are at all reluctant to begin sharing. (Usually they are not!)

After our class sharing time, I send students home with their interview worksheets to talk with various family members about their memories. I usually recommend that, if possible, they talk to at least two different relatives. (I have had students who, for one reason or another, have not been able to talk with anyone in their families, in which case I suggest they just practice the assignment by talking to an older person they know. I reassure them that the next phase of this exercise will be more appropriate to their situation.)

Finally, I ask students to take one small detail they know about their family history and, like Maxine Hong Kingston and Toni Morrison, imagine the rest of the story in any way they'd like. Perhaps all one boy knows is that his great-great grandparents came to this country during the potato famine, or a girl knows only that her ancestors were Mayan Indians. Given just that little information, I encourage them to imagine who they think these people were.

Themes and Variations

These reflections on our personal histories can become the basis for extensive research projects. In imagining their stories, students may want to collect factual information and use that knowledge in writing their stories. Or teachers may want to focus the interviews around a particular topic—immigration, for instance—and link it to a historical study.

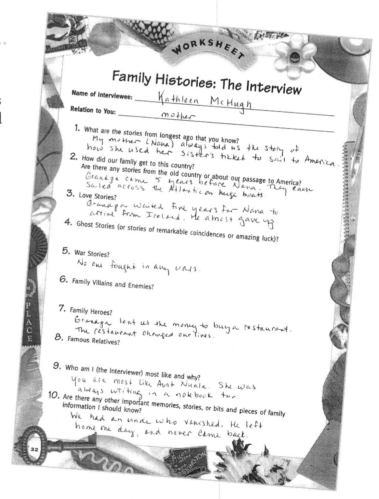

Family Histories: The Interview

Name of Interviewee: _____

Relation to You: _____

1. What are the stories from longest ago that you know?

2. How did our family get to this country?
   Are there any stories from the old country or about our passage to America?

3. Love Stories?

4. Ghost Stories (or stories of remarkable coincidences or amazing luck)?

5. War Stories?

6. Family Villains and Enemies?

7. Family Heroes?

8. Famous Relatives?

9. Who am I (the interviewer) most like and why?

10. Are there any other important memories, stories, or bits and pieces of family information I should know?

Shaping the Piece

Sunday was always my favorite day of the week. I would to the smells of a ... My father always ... on Sunday — it ...

Works in Progress

To begin the process of revision, I have students choose one piece from their initial work that they would like to present to the class as a work in progress. It will probably be something they've developed from the initial activities. Sometimes a completely new idea will emerge as a result of having looked at so many topics and having to share writing with the class. What is important about this presentation is simply this: It is a work in progress and not a finished piece.

My goal is to cultivate in students an attitude of artistic openness. To that end, I have them present process logs along with their pieces—accounts of how they have worked on the pieces thus far and of what they would like to do with the writing in the future.

Given enough time, we do this as a whole class. Students learn from each other's work and are frequently inspired to do better writing when they hear what their classmates are up to. Later, however, I send everybody to their reading/writing groups to continue the sharing. To structure students' reflections about their work, I have them use the PROCESS LOG WORKSHEET. And so that their peers provide them with useful feedback, I provide a PEER RESPONSE WORKSHEET as well.

As always, throughout the process, students have been sharing pieces with each other—at the end of class, during an activity, and so on. Again, it's important to bring our writing to a supportive audience *while we are working on it*. It's important to talk about our pieces so we can discover new ways of saying what we want to say. It is also important to mark the transitions in our writing process. Now is the time to submit a formal proposal, to present the work we've done thus far and think about what else we'd like to do with it.

The following exercises help students begin to realize what their pieces are about, what they really mean. This is where the memories collected through the past weeks become transformed into memoir, where the clay we collected is shaped and sculpted into a work of art.

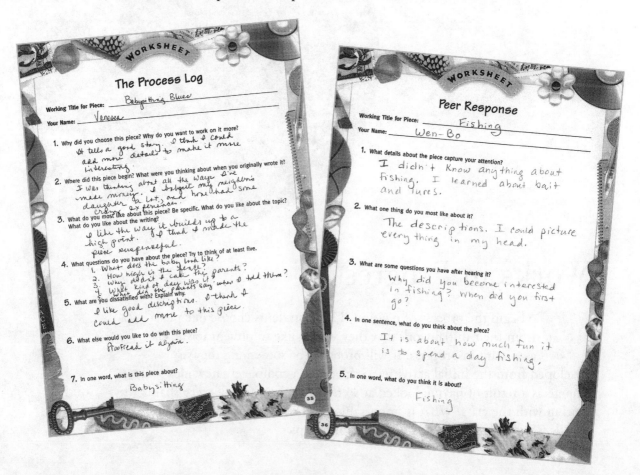

The Process Log

Working Title for Piece: _____

Your Name: _____

1. Why did you choose this piece? Why do you want to work on it more?

2. Where did this piece begin? What were you thinking about when you originally wrote it?

3. What do you most like about this piece? Be specific. What do you like about the topic? What do you like about the writing?

4. What questions do you have about the piece? Try to think of at least five.

5. What are you dissatisfied with? Explain why.

6. What else would you like to do with this piece?

7. In one word, what is this piece about?

Peer Response

Working Title for Piece: _____

Your Name: _____

1. What details about the piece capture your attention?

2. What one thing do you most like about it?

3. What are some questions you have after hearing it?

4. In one sentence, what do you think about the piece?

5. In one word, what do you think it is about?

Some Thoughts on Revision

Revision is one of the most difficult habits to instill in young writers. They reach the end of the page, put down their pencils, and announce, "I'm done!" How difficult it is to shake our heads, hand back the pens, and respond, "Oh no, you are just beginning."

Revision often feels like a chore—correcting punctuation and spelling, the endless copying over (if we are not lucky enough to be working on computers), changing this word and that word. In fact, however, that is not revision—it is copyediting, that final process before a piece is ready for publication. Real revision is a journey, an exploration into the heart of what we are trying to say. If our discoveries are to be real, we cannot possibly imagine them at the outset. We do not know what we will find out.

As we begin the revision process, I tell my students that we are setting out on an adventure with our pieces. What we have already written will not disappear while we travel. Just because we go somewhere else, we will not lose what we already have. Like our homes, we can always return at any time. This is a great fear of young writers—they love the piece they've chosen to work on and are terrified that if they change it in any way, they will not be able to recover what they originally had. Well, it's right there in their notebooks! So why worry? (NOTE: If students are working on computers, it is important to have them keep hard copies of all their work.)

On the journey of revision students will visit many new places with the activities we offer. At the end of their explorations, some will decide to completely redecorate their original homes, some will just bring back a few souvenirs, and others may decide to pack up and move to a new country. I evaluate them on how open they are to the journey itself. Do they try all the different ways of exploring their pieces? Do they push themselves to look at their work in new ways? As with their notebooks, I am interested in their commitment to the process and not just the quality of the final piece of writing.

A few years ago, my husband was working on a proposal for a book he wanted to write. Month after month, he labored over it, exploring what he really wanted to say. When he finished the proposal, he would give himself a little time away from it and then look at it again. "Not quite right," he'd say and push himself to go deeper into the topic. Finally, after almost a year of work, he was done. He gave the proposal to his agent who sent it off to a dozen different publishers. Not one of them was interested in it.

My husband was devastated. But, then, because he is a writer, he sat back down to work again. Now, finally, he knew what he'd been trying to get at all along. He wrote a proposal for what, on its surface, would seem to be a completely different book. But it was like the butterfly that can fly only after the caterpillar has been crawling around eating all spring. My husband wrote that proposal in two weeks, and sold it in a day.

MINI-LESSON *11*

Magnets

In his memoir *Boy*, Roald Dahl tells a series of incredibly painful stories—about the death of his father, getting caned for a practical joke, having his adenoids removed without anesthesia, more canings, a lanced boil. It goes on and on. He doesn't dwell on the idyllic summers in Norway or on his adventures with his many siblings. Naturally, Dahl can't help but be funny, and he punctuates the scenes of agony with uproarious accounts of practical jokes, but ultimately this is a memoir about what one little boy endured at the hands of some pretty insensitive grown-ups.

Memoirs have themes—ideas that connect various episodes and details in a life. I like to think of the themes as magnets which pick up certain moments and episodes and ignore nearly everything else, for memoir does not tell everything. Instead, it tries to find a strand of meaning in all that has happened to us.

Magnets Activity

Using their process logs and the feedback they received from their peers, have students identify some magnet words or themes from their pieces. Dahl's words might have been "suffering" or "horrible grown-ups." It is helpful to generate four to six words as not all of them will be equally powerful.

Then, using the magnet words, students read through all the material in their notebooks from the earlier activities. They should list all the episodes, details, moments, and stories their magnet words pick up. A magnet list might look something like this:

Working Title: **When we left Boston for the seashore, I was five.**

Magnet Word: **Moving**

※ changing schools in third grade and not knowing the teachers

※ the airplane trip to Washington when I was eight

※ watching our new house being built and wondering which would be my bedroom

※ a beautiful sunset (the sun *moving* through the sky)

※ my grandmother homesick for England

38

MINI-LESSON 12

Wondering

So what was it all about? I used to ask myself.

from *Boy*, by Roald Dahl

Writing memoir is about asking questions and not just telling what happened. At the end of his book, Roald Dahl does a lot of wondering about all the terrible things these grown-ups did to him. Who were these people? What do their actions tell him about the universe, about God? His attempts at answering these questions take him on a surprising journey.

Wondering Activity

This activity is about asking questions about the pieces we are working on. The objective, initially, is to ask as many questions as possible in the hope that a couple of them will lead us to some interesting insights. The kinds of questions to ask include the following:

- **General questions about what happened and why:**

  "Why me?"
  "Why then?"

- **Questions to the people involved in the memoir:**

  "Why didn't you call me that day?"
  "What were you really thinking when you said that?"

- **Questions that take nothing for granted:**

  "Why was the sky blue that day?"

- **Questions to yourself:**

  "How come I never cried about what happened?"

- **What if…:**

  "What if we had never moved?"

The next step is to choose one or two questions and play with all possible answers. Remember that there are no right or wrong answers, just interesting ways of thinking about something that happened to us.

Panoramas

The great, dark trees of the Big Woods stood all around the house, and beyond them were other trees and beyond them were more trees. As far as a man could go to the north in a day, or a week, or a whole month, there was nothing but woods.

from *Little House in the Big Woods*,
by Laura Ingalls Wilder

Once a student of mine was writing a memoir, the centerpiece of which was a long account of some very dangerous rock climbing he had done. Meticulously, sparing not even the smallest possible detail, he described each outcropping of rock as he edged forward. But when I asked him to describe the mountain and the remarkable terrain he was in, he looked at me aghast and said, "Ms. Finn, if I'd looked around I'd have fallen!"

When we are fully engaged in a moment, we may not want to (or be able to) take our noses away from the rock in front of us. When we are *writing* about that moment, however, we need to remember we have the freedom to look around, to note everything, to see whatever we want.

Laura Ingalls Wilder opens her memoir by letting us see the vast wilderness surrounding her little house. In *An American Childhood*, Annie Dillard looks into the untamed territory of Pittsburgh before it became the industrial town she grew up in. And in Jon Krakauer's best-selling memoir about climbing Mount Everest, he first offers us the terrible majesty of the Himalayas, seen from a bird's eye view, before recounting his own tragic ascent. It's important to explore the meanings *inside* a piece, but we need to open our eyes to its place in the bigger picture as well.

Panoramas Activity

Students begin this activity by deciding on one specific location in their memoir to look at. It should be a place that's important to the piece, preferably at its heart.

Next I give students huge pieces of white paper—as big as I can find—and ask them to draw tiny representations of their scenes at the center. It goes without saying that the focus of this activity is not artistic skill, and I usually tell students that we will do this very quickly—in a minute or so.

The rest of the period (and frequently the homework) is filling in what surrounds the scenes. Some students are very precise and will draw their houses and then detailed maps of their whole neighborhood. Others will be comprehensive and show the whole solar system and the Milky Way. There's no right way to do this, but students should be encouraged to fill the whole piece of paper.

Finally, students should share their pictures with each other and work on translating them into writing. Some will want to start in the center and move toward the edges of the paper; others will want to start far away and move in closer and closer to themselves. They should include every detail that they have drawn but also feel free to add things as they write that might not have been in their drawings.

MINI-LESSON 14

Close-ups

My brother's ears are round, like dried apricots, or like the ears of the green-tinged, oval-headed aliens from outer space he draws with his colored pencils. Around and over his round ears and down the back of his neck his hair, dark blonde and straight, grows in thick wisps. He resists haircuts.

from *Cats Eye*, by Margaret Atwood

Just as we sometimes need to lift up our heads to see the big picture when we are writing, we need to remember the value of close-ups as well. "God is in the details," said a famous architect, and as writers, it is important that we look closely at what we are writing about.

Close-ups Activity

With this mini-lesson, I do more directed teaching initially. First, I write a sentence on the board and ask the students to visualize what I have written. Usually, I will write,

The cat is fat.

Then I call on students and have them tell me what that sentence evokes in their imaginations. "I saw my black and white cat named Titanic," says one. "I saw Garfield," says another.

"That's interesting," I tell them, "because I saw my orange cat, Pudge, who weighs just under twenty pounds and sleeps all day with his nose pressed against his food bowl. Sometimes, when he is eating, he reaches out

a paw to cover the other food bowl so his brother can't eat. He always has bits of cat food clinging to his whiskers." The challenge of writing is to take the pictures we have in our heads and offer our readers enough details so they can see the same picture we do.

Now the students practice noticing details. First, I might ask them to describe their school lunches and notice as many details as they can. I remind them to use all their senses and look carefully. Next, I might put some flowers or an interesting rock on a table for them to describe.

Finally, I ask the students to isolate two or three things that they feel are important to their memoirs and to look at them close up. "Be specific, not abstract," I say. "Work at describing what you see so that I can see it too."

(Troubleshooting)

"But my piece isn't about anything…"

Some students will resist seeing anything other than the events as they actually experienced them. "It just happened, that's why it's important," they say. They don't have any questions, they can't find any memories that connect, they seem not to want to do any more work on their pieces at all. What should you do?

Often, these students have chosen topics that have *too* much meaning for them, memories that are, in fact, too recent and too powerful to write about. Students do not have any distance yet on these experiences and are thus resistant to exploring them.

Once a student of mine was writing about the recent death of his father. While he was very attached to the piece, he didn't want to revise it at all. Of course not! He wanted only to hold on to what he had just lost. My advice to him was to keep the piece as he had written it so far, but then try to write about his father in a less immediate way—to find out stories about his father's boyhood from relatives.

If a student does not want to work on a different topic (one they may be able to engage with more deeply), I try to find ways to help them create distance in the pieces they are working on. They might try writing in the third person (as if they were writing about someone else). They might try injecting the work with fantastical or magical elements. Or they might, as did my student, rely on someone else's memories rather than their own.

MINI-LESSON 16

Fast-Forward

When we are writing about something that happened to us, it can be difficult to remember that not *all* of the details are equally important. Particularly when students have been focusing on generating material, there comes a time when they have to read their pieces and think about any parts they would fast-forward over if they were watching it on video. One way of fast-forwarding in writing is by summarizing a series of events in a single sentence or two, as shown below:

We all got in the car and drove out the driveway and then we had to stop at the gas station. My little sister wanted to get a soda. And then we got on the highway and we drove for like six hours and I slept for a while and then played with my gameboy. We stopped once for dinner and I had chicken nuggets. It was pretty boring but then we got to the lake where I had my adventure.

How about…

After a tedious ride in the car, we arrived at the lake.

Fast-Forward Activity

Students can practice fast-forwarding with the excerpt on the worksheet. First they should read it over and decide which part does not seem to be central to the theme of the memoir. Then after underlining the passage they feel is not important, they should try summarizing the information contained within the excerpt in a single sentence. I often find it helpful to have students discuss which lines they've chosen to fast-forward over and why and then share their summarizing sentences.

   Now students should turn to their own work. Are there any places where the writing drags? They will probably want to discuss their work with classmates and hear their insights as well. It is important to remind students that their writing may be quite concise in place and therefore in no need of fast-forwarding.

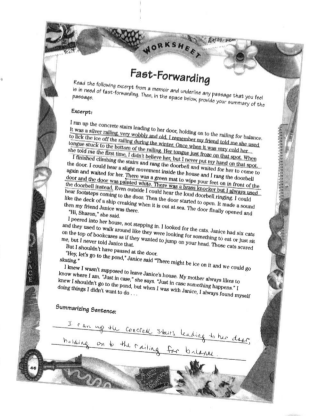

Fast-Forwarding

Read the following excerpt from a memoir and underline any passage that you feel is in need of fast-forwarding. Then, in the space below, provide your summary of the passage.

Excerpt:

I ran up the concrete stairs leading to her door, holding on to the railing for balance. It was a silver railing, very wobbly and old. I remember my friend told me she used to lick the ice off the railing during the winter. Once when it was very cold her tongue stuck to the bottom of the railing. Her tongue just froze on that spot. When she told me the first time, I didn't believe her, but I never put my hand on that spot.

I finished climbing the stairs and rang the doorbell and waited for her to come to the door. I could hear a slight movement inside the house and I rang the doorbell again and waited for her. There was a green mat to wipe your feet on in front of the door and the door was painted white. There was a brass knocker but I always used the doorbell instead. Even outside I could hear the loud doorbell ringing. I could hear footsteps coming to the door. Then the door started to open. It made a sound like the deck of a ship creaking when it is out at sea. The door finally opened and then my friend Janice was there.

"Hi, Sharon," she said.

I peered into her house, not stepping in. I looked for the cats. Janice had six cats and they used to walk around like they were looking for something to eat or just sit on the top of bookcases as if they wanted to jump on your head. Those cats scared me, but I never told Janice that.

But I shouldn't have paused at the door.

"Hey, let's go to the pond," Janice said "There might be ice on it and we could go skating."

I knew I wasn't supposed to leave Janice's house. My mother always likes to know where I am. "Just in case," she says. "Just in case something happens." I knew I shouldn't go to the pond, but when I was with Janice, I always found myself doing things I didn't want to do . . .

Summarizing Sentence:

_____

_____

Slow Motion

Then I hit him. I balled my fist and swung, and when my knuckles landed—thock—against his chin bone, I was as surprised as when my stone hit Johnny Seeton.

As punches go, it was dainty, more tap than wallop, my intention being to match a punch's form, not force. I'm sure that physically, he barely felt it. But a punch has a double impact, as I was about to learn, and only the first lands on the chin. Joey's eyes widened. He stood staring at me with such wild astonishment that I knew at once he had not, not in a million years, been asking for it.

from *Knots in My Yo-Yo String,*
by Jerry Spinelli

Just as students can spend too much time describing events that are of little relevance to the heart of their pieces, they can sometimes speed right over the most important moments of their memoir. In his chapter "War," Jerry Spinelli quickly mentions his interest in comic books and stories about battles but spends almost two paragraphs describing the moment of impact when he punched Joey Stackhouse. Why? Because it was the moment that changed forever what he thought about fighting.

Slow Motion Activity

Students should read their pieces in groups and decide which is the most important moment in each of their memoirs. Have they given it enough time and enough weight? Could they slow it down a little more so the reader has time to experience its full importance for the writer?

Some students will say that they have more than one moment that is important. That's fine. However, every moment in the whole piece shouldn't be of equal significance. Both this exercise and the preceding one are designed to help young writers recognize that their writing can (and should) have different rhythms, different weights.

MINI-LESSON 18

One Last Look

What makes a painter an artist is a willingness to look at something and to see in it what no one else has noticed. Revision literally means "to look at something again," and it can be valuable for students as they finish the drafting process to take one last careful look at what they are writing about. Sometimes it is only after we have seen and written all the things we already know that we can at last be surprised.

One Last Look Activity

To practice looking more carefully, I take out an ordinary object like an apple and show it to the class. "Look at it," I say, "Notice what no one else notices."

Then I pass the apple around the room and have each student notice one thing about the apple. Each must say something that no one else has yet said. Naturally, as the apple travels, students' observations become more and more creative.

When each student has noticed one thing about the apple, I then announce that I am going to pass it around again, going back the way it came. Each student must recognize one more thing about it that no one else has noticed. It's a challenge!

Sometimes students will have neglected the obvious, and I will point out to them things like its color and shape. At other times, they will need prodding to think about the object more deeply, to consider where it came from, where it's going, to connect it to other apples they have seen or tasted, or to imagine things about it that only they could know.

Now students should turn to their memoirs, reread them, and then spend some time visualizing what they have written. What obvious things have they forgotten to say? What details have they overlooked? What other memories suddenly feel connected to these? What questions do they suddenly find themselves asking? What last writing do they need to do for this piece?

Frames

Laura Ingalls Wilder presents the events of *Little House in the Big Woods* as though they happened over the course of one year. She tells different stories from each season and ends with autumn where she had begun. In actuality, she lived in the big woods at two different times in her childhood but found it more artistic to present her stories as an organized whole. Just as painters like to put borders and frames around their artwork to make them look finished or stand out more, writers will often use devices of time or place to structure their memoirs.

They may use the rhythm of the year, the seasons, to organize their stories, or they may follow the course of one season as does Robert McCloskey in *Time of Wonder*. He begins with the gentle spring rains and ends with the first of fall's hurricanes. Similarly, a writer will sometimes open a narrative in the morning and conclude it with the coming of darkness.

Just as time can frame a story, so can place. Sandra Cisneros jumps all around in time but keeps the events on Mango Street. In his hilarious memoirs of his family, Gerald Durrell has everything happen on the Greek Island of Corfu. Did it? Maybe not, but he keeps the story unified and the seemingly disparate stories connected.

Sometimes the frames can be more personal. In a memoir about her beloved sister, a student of mine opened with going to see her in the hospital when she was born and ended with going to see her at the hospital when she was terminally ill.

Frames Activity

Students can experiment with putting frames around their memoirs. First they should try one of time, then of place, and finally one of a unifying event. What changes would each frame make to the piece? Would it highlight anything that wasn't as noticeable before? Or would it seem like too much, like some big gaudy gold frame around a delicate watercolor? Frames work when they complement the paintings inside them. They don't work when they overpower the art.

Students need only imagine and discuss the different possible frames. Then, if they find one that really works, they can use it for their memoirs. Often students actually have bits and pieces of their frames already in place and just have to enlarge them to make the frames more effective.

MINI-LESSON 20

Sequences

By now students have memoirs—they have transformative moments, stories, descriptions, and, most importantly, connecting ideas or themes. They may even have found framing devices. The next consideration is how to organize and present all this material within those frames. If they wish, students may simply follow a chronology—first this happened, then this, then this. But even when we are narrating a story among friends, we are rarely that linear. We realize we left out some important background material so we jump way back in time; we seem to digress as we tell the whole story of one of the characters; even before we are done telling our tale, we are emphasizing its importance to us right now. There are many different ways to sequence a piece of writing.

Sequences Activity

First have students investigate all the different memoirs they have been reading—the picture books and the longer chapter books they have been sharing in their groups. What are some of the different ways the writers organize their information?

Some writers start with the most important event and then go back in time to explain what led up to it. Others start way back in history and then end with the most important moment. Still others jump around, beginning in the middle of things and leaving us up in the air at the end.

After students have noticed and discussed the different ways writers have sequenced their memoirs, they should look at how they have currently put their own piece of writing together. Would they like to change the sequence of events and images in any way?

One way students can experiment with the organization of their pieces is to literally cut them up and shuffle them around in different order. Have students copy their pieces or print out an extra copy on the computer, cut it into scenes or paragraphs, and then play with all different ways of organizing the scenes. They should be very playful and try lots of different patterns.

Have students discovered any new ways of organizing their pieces? If not, they still have their originals to return to. If so, they can now make changes to the pieces.

———— ⧜ ————

But Laura lay awake a little while, listening to Pa's fiddle softly playing and to the lonely sound of the wind in the Big Woods. She looked at Pa sitting on the bench by the hearth, the firelight gleaming on his brown hair and beard and glistening on the honey-brown fiddle. She looked at Ma, gently rocking and knitting.

She thought to herself, "This is now."

She was glad that the cozy house, and Pa and Ma and the firelight and the music, were now. They could not be forgotten, she thought, because now is now. It can never be a long time ago.

from *Little House in the Big Woods*
by Laura Ingalls Wilder

My mother had promised my brother and me a trip to the beach if the weather was good. My brother and I anxiously listened to the weather report on the news.

The sky was bright blue as my mother backed the car out of the driveway.

For the first hour the sun was a bright, shining disk in the sky. We swam for close to an hour.

CHAPTER

Sharing Our Writing with an Audience

What motivates me to do my very best writing is the knowledge of what I will be doing with my final piece. Will I be entering a contest, or trying to have it published in a magazine? Will I be offering it as a gift to someone I love? At the beginning of a project, I try to forget about my audience and let go of all my self-consciousness and self-criticism as a writer—I want to listen to my heart. As my piece nears completion, however, my awareness of an audience returns and inspires me to clean up loose ends, solve little problems, and make my writing presentable. I want my audience to hear what I have to say and not be distracted by peculiar spellings, strange usage, or awkward punctuation. If I care enough about the fate of a piece, I'll read it over a hundred times to find any last mistake.

Copyediting and Proofreading

Cleaning up a piece of writing does not need to be drudgery. In fact, I try to allow enough time so that we can have fun with copyediting and proofreading and not feel too rushed. Not only am I helping the students ready their pieces for publication, but I want to teach them valuable skills as well.

It's important for students to know that all published writing is copyedited and proofread—not just by their authors, but nearly always by professional proofreaders and editors. The goal is not simply to be able to do it all for yourself but to know how to use your available resources. For instance, I am not a great speller, so I know I have to use the spell check. But I also use the keen eye of a former editor and spelling bee champ—my husband. In like manner, I have students work in groups to polish their pieces.

Depending on what work I have done previously with students on copyediting, I may do some mini-lessons on clarifying confusing passages, paragraphing, tightening language, playing with sentence variety, active versus passive verbs, and so on. As I like to keep our work connected to what actually happens in the professional writing world, I make sure each of them has a blue pencil and I teach them copyediting notation. Any number of books on writing have both exercises and information on how to help students develop these skills.

When it comes time to correct spelling, usage, and punctuation, I create challenges. One day, we focus on spelling and see which group will be the first to present all their pieces to me without a single spelling error. Dictionaries are out, computers are on, and everyone is carefully scanning each other's work. I refuse to point out a misspelled word or provide a correct spelling. I only let them know if there are still mistakes in a piece. When one group succeeds, I assign its members to the remaining groups to help them finish the challenge.

We do the same for usage and punctuation—although, if I can, I like to take a few days for each of these areas and focus on some specific problem areas that the class may have.

When I receive students' final papers, they will not need any corrections. They have already done that work, and they have done it themselves. After all, polishing our pieces is not really about filling in the corrections the teacher has indicated, but developing our own awareness of what might need straightening up.

Publishing Opportunities

In my classroom I try to create opportunities for my students' work that will inspire them to do their best. What follows is a list of possibilities for publishing and celebrating students' work in the classroom:

1. Writing Contests

Various magazines, educational groups, and writing organizations offer yearly contests that accept memoirs (sometimes they will ask for nonfiction or essays).

2. Magazines

Many magazines, both children's and adults', accept student work for publication. *Merlyn's Pen, Cricket, Stone Soup,* and so on. *The Sun,* a literary magazine out of North Carolina, regularly solicits memoirs from its readers. As memoir is an increasingly popular genre, it is hard these days to open any magazine without finding some examples of it.

3. Anthologies

Create a book that includes all of the students' memoirs. It can be illustrated, have a table of contents, a fabulous cover, and information about each of the authors. From year to year, my students have created these books, and they have become part of our classroom library, available for the pleasure and study of other classes. I always try to make the books as beautiful as possible and provide each student with a copy.

Ms. Everett's Class Anthology of Memoirs

4. Picture Books

I have had great success in making picture books of our memoirs for younger siblings and the lower grades. The writing in many picture books is superb and worthy of emulation. Interestingly, working on the pictures often encourages students to do more work on their texts. A number of different bookbinding techniques are possible, but the materials can be as simple as a stapler, contact paper, and some cardboard. If possible, scheduling a reading of their books to younger schoolmates can be a wonderful celebration of students' final work.

5. Formal Readings

Even if we have sent off our work to a magazine or created a classroom anthology, I like to honor the students' final work with a formal reading. We send out invitations to friends and family, decorate the room, provide refreshments, and set up a podium with a microphone. I have students practice reading their pieces aloud many times in advance (and, yes, some of them are a little scared), and many are still revising just moments before going on. Just like real writers!

Final Evaluations

By the time students have finished their memoirs, I have spent a lot of time with each of their pieces. We have talked at length about its strengths and weaknesses, explored ideas together, corrected it together. What does there remain for me to say about it?

In my final evaluation, I like both to reflect back to the students what they have learned about writing with this project and also to honor their individual pieces. I ask students to write their own final evaluation of their work and to give themselves grades. Then I write them letters responding to their insights—or, occasionally, their lack of insights. In many ways, the most powerful final evaluation, the moment of truth, is the publishing itself. No grade is as powerful as an acceptance letter, or a second grader rushing up to gush, "That was the best story I've ever heard in my whole life," or a fellow classmate saying, "I wish I could write like you."

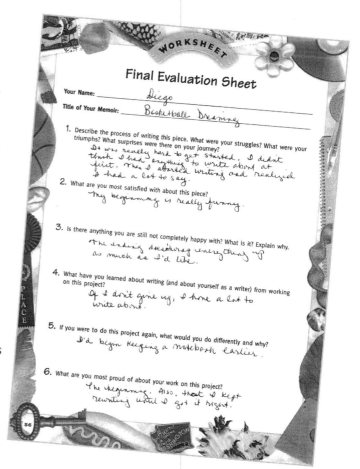

WORKSHEET

Final Evaluation Sheet

Your Name: _Diego_

Title of Your Memoir: _Basketball Dreaming_

1. Describe the process of writing this piece. What were your struggles? What were your triumphs? What surprises were there on your journey?
   It was really hard to get started. I didn't think I had anything to write about at first. When I started writing and realized I had a lot to say.

2. What are you most satisfied with about this piece?
   My beginning is really funny.

3. Is there anything you are still not completely happy with? What is it? Explain why.
   The ending doesn't wrap everything up as much as I'd like.

4. What have you learned about writing (and about yourself as a writer) from working on this project?
   If I don't give up, I have a lot to write about.

5. If you were to do this project again, what would you do differently and why?
   I'd begin keeping a notebook earlier.

6. What are you most proud of about your work on this project?
   The beginning. Also, that I kept rewriting until I got it right.

56

Final Evaluation Sheet

Your Name: _____

Title of Your Memoir: _____

1. Describe the process of writing this piece. What were your struggles? What were your triumphs? What surprises were there on your journey?

2. What are you most satisfied with about this piece?

3. Is there anything you are still not completely happy with? What is it? Explain why.

4. What have you learned about writing (and about yourself as a writer) from working on this project?

5. If you were to do this project again, what would you do differently and why?

6. What are you most proud of about your work on this project?

Sample Memoirs

The following two memoirs are for class discussion and study. Each organizes different episodes and moments from a life around a theme, and it may be interesting for students to look at both how the writers have organized their scenes and what kinds of details they have chosen to share. As memoir writers themselves, what do students notice about what these writers are doing and why?

My Name

by Sandra Cisneros

In English my name means hope. In Spanish it means too many letters. It means sadness, it means waiting. It is like the number nine. A muddy color. It is the Mexican records my father plays on Sunday mornings when he is shaving, songs like sobbing.

It was my great-grandmother's name and now it is mine. She was a horse woman too, born like me in the Chinese Year of the horse—which is supposed to be bad luck if you're born female—but I think this is a Chinese lie because the Chinese, like the Mexicans, don't like their women strong.

My great-grandmother. I would've liked to have known her, a wild horse of a woman, so wild she wouldn't marry. Until my great-grandfather threw a sack over her head and carried her off. Just like that, as if she were a fancy chandelier. That's the way she did it.

And the story goes she never forgave him. She looked out the window her whole life, the way so many women sit their sadness on an elbow. I wonder if she made the best with what she got or was she sorry because she couldn't be all the things she wanted to be. Esperanza. I have inherited her name, but I don't want to inherit her place by the window.

At school they say my name funny as if the syllables were made out of tin and hurt the roof of your mouth. But in Spanish my name is made out of a softer something, like silver, not quite as thick as my sister's name—Magdalena—which is uglier than mine. Magdalena who at least can come home and become Nenny. But I am always Esperanza.

I would like to baptize myself under a new name, a name more like the real me, the one nobody sees. Esperanza as Lisandra or Maritza or Zeze the X. Yes. Something like Zeze the X will do.

"WAR"

from *Knots in My Yo-Yo String*

by Jerry Spinelli

I hate war. But when I was little, I loved it. War was a game, guns were toys, death an amusement ride. The first card game I ever played was called war.

I also played with little green soldiers, maybe two inches high. I loved their perfect, tiny helmets that reminded me of cereal bowls. Even the faces of the soldiers were perfect and green. Their tiny mouths and eyes were forever locked into a battlefield moment that I could only imagine.

I read G.I. Joe and Combat Kelly comic books. Then, down at the creek, I would poke a stick into the powdery bottom silt, pop it upward, and go "Boom!" I pretended the resulting brown underwater cloud was an atomic bomb explosion.

And of course, I played war with my friends. Beyond the dead end, there were two major arsenals: the stone piles and the spear field. The stone piles were on the other side of the tracks, between the main dump and the creek. There were five of them, each about ten feet high. The piles no doubt belonged to a construction company, but as far as we dead-end kids were concerned, they were there strictly in answer to our instinct to fling a stone.

Yet the one real stone battle I recall happened not there but at the creek (another inexhaustible source of stones; it wasn't called Stony Creek for nothing). We divided ourselves into two platoons and took up positions on either side of the creek. We loaded up and fired away.

The creek at that point was hardly wider than an alleyway. Across the water Johnny Seeton was firing from behind a tree. I waited till he poked his head out. He was looking right at me. I fired. I was aiming to hit him in the eyebrow. This is not as malicious as it sounds, for we were only playing at war—we were pretending, and everybody knew you didn't get hurt pretending. Besides, Johnny Seeton was one of my two best friends. And double-besides, who ever actually hit what they were aiming at?

The stone hit him in the eyebrow.

He screamed. He wouldn't stop screaming. Blood streamed down his face. He galloped across the water, ignoring stepping stones, screamed up the creek bank, and screamed all the way home. As for me, pretend did not give way to horror instantly. For several seconds of fanciful confusion, as Johnny Seeton thrashed wildly past me, I felt surprised that our relationship as best friends did not seem to count in this matter, as if a stone thrown by me should hurt him less.

Neither Johnny nor his parents ever said anything to me about the incident. They didn't have to. The two-week patch on Johnny's eye punished me every day.

Spears were safer.

Go to the dead end, turn left, walk up the tracks past Red Hill and the other, smaller dump, climb the trackside bluff, and you were in the spear field—so named for the plants growing there. Strip one of them of its leaves, and you were left with a sturdy four-foot high stalk straight as a pool cue. Pluck it from the ground, shake off the root dirt, and bring on the enemy.

As I passed through the grade-school years, war became less about machine-gun chatter and spectacular explosions and more about people.

I read about war, about the bodies of soldiers, even enemy soldiers, whose lifeless hands clutched photographs of loved ones back home.

I read of the torture of captive troops. I especially cringed over the fingernail torture, in which a pair of pliers pulled out the victim's fingernails, slowly, one by one. Such things happened to spies and to people who knew too many secrets. I resolved that if I was ever in a war, I would be a dumb nonspy.

But I could not resolve not to be a soldier. Every passing day, every February 1—the date of my birth—prodded me closer to the ominous cloud that hung over my future. It was called the draft, and it meant that when I (and all other boys deemed healthy enough) got out of high school or college, I would have to join the armed forces whether I wanted to or not.

As if to prepare me, my daydreams placed me in grim wartime situations. I saw myself, apparently a failure at avoiding secrets, in the hands of enemy interrogators.

"Tell us," they growl.

"Never," I say firmly, for I am a good American soldier.

Then I feel the pliers grip the end of the nail on my right index finger, and cold sweat pours from me, and I feel the tug of the pliers and then the pain begins—and I sing. I sing like the Vienna Boys' Choir. I empty my head like a box of cornflakes. I tell them everything from our deepest military secrets to my shoe size.

And I anguish. Because, though I realize this is only a daydream, I am afraid that if such a thing ever really happens, I will play my part poorly. I am afraid that I will crack during torture. I am ashamed that I cannot measure up to a captive spy I once read about, whose lips were still sealed after losing all ten fingernails.

Sometimes in my fearful fantasies my captors bypassed torture and simply marched me out to the firing squad. But I never got shot. Even as six rifle sights met at my trembling heart— "Ready! Aim!"— I call out to the commanding officer, "Wait a minute!"

The commanding officer pauses.

"There's something you don't know. If you shoot me, you'll never find out."

The officer calls off the guns. He expects me to divulge vital military secrets, but the information I offer is purely personal. I tell him something about his wife, his family back home, something he could never have known without me. He is overcome with gratitude. He dismisses the firing squad. And I have discovered something: Words can save me.

Despite all the attention I paid to warfare, I was never in a real fight. Around sixth grade this began to bother me, I saw other kids flailing and clubbing, tearing each other's shirts to shreds, trading bloody noses, and I said to myself, "Hey, why not me?" I began to feel deprived because my right hand had never known the feel of fist on chin. I felt a growing need to hit somebody.

But who? I could think of no one I wanted to hit. And apparently nobody wanted to hit me. Every day I walked to and from school unchallenged. I was a burr in no one's saddle. A likable bloke.

However, the prospect of going through life punchless was too strong to ignore. I looked around my classroom. Who was as small as I, or better yet, even smaller? Who was unlikely to hit me back? Who needed hitting?

There was only one answer: Joey Stackhouse.

Joey Stackhouse was skinny. Mash down his blond pompadour and he was maybe half an inch shorter than I. He had a narrow, foxy face. But his main feature was teeth. He was a walking warning against not brushing. When he smiled, you found yourself looking at all the colors in your crayon box. Plus his clothes were shabby.

For several days I hung close to Joey, alert for an offending remark or gesture. He remained obstinately harmless, as friendly as ever. It became clear that I myself would have to manufacture the momentum for the punch.

I worked myself into a snit. I convinced myself that anybody with teeth like that was asking for it. One day he walked home with me after school. We were on the 700 block of George Street, close to my house. I picked a fight with him, accused him of something, I don't remember what. Then I hit him. I balled my fist and swung, and when my knuckles landed— thock—against his chin bone, I was as surprised as when my stone hit Johnny Seeton.

As punches go, it was dainty, more tap than wallop, my intention being to match a punch's form, not force. I'm sure that, physically, he barely felt it. But a punch has a double impact, as I was about to learn, and only the first lands on the chin. Joey's eyes widened. He stood there staring at me with such wild astonishment that I knew at once he had not, not in a million years, been asking for it. He started to cry. He blurted out, "Why'd you do that?" and ran back down George Street.

If ever I had notions of becoming a warrior, they died that day as I turned the other way and walked home alone. It has been more than forty years since I hit Joey Stackhouse—the first and last person I ever punched—and it remains the only taste of war I ever needed.

Bibliography

Picture Books

While most older students are beyond reading picture books, the value of these books in the writing workshop classroom is that they allow students to experience and study many complete texts. While students might be able to finish only one or two chapter books during the genre study, they can read scores of picture books—and they can reread them and study the writers' techniques and styles as well.

Always Grandma, by Vaunda Michaux Nelson (Putnam, 1988).*

The Art Lesson, by Tomie de Paola (Putnam, 1989).

Christmas Tree Memories, by Aliki (HarperCollins, 1991).

Grandfather's Journey, by Allen Say (Houghton Mifflin, 1993).

Grandpa, by Barbara Borack (Harper and Row, 1967).*

Home Place, by Crescent Dragonwagon (Macmillan, 1990).

Miss Rumphius, by Barbara Cooney (Viking, 1982).

My Rotten Redheaded Older Brother, by Patricia Polacco (Simon and Schuster, 1994).

Nana Upstairs and Nana Downstairs, by Tomie de Paola (Puffin, 1978).

No Star Nights, by Anna Egan Smucker (Knopf, 1994).

Time of Wonder, by Robert McCloskey (Viking, 1957).

The Rag Coat, by Lauren Mills (Little Brown, 1991).

Thunder Cake, by Patricia Polacco (Putnam, 1997).

Tom, by Tomie de Paola (Putnam, 1993).

Uncle Vova's Tree, by Patricia Polacco (Philomel, 1989).

When I Was Nine, by James Stevenson (Greenwillow Books, 1986).

When I Was Young in The Mountains, by Cynthia Rylant (Dutton, 1982).

Chapter Books

Boy: Tales of Childhood, by Roald Dahl (Puffin, 1986).

A Day No Pigs Would Die, by Robert Newton Peck (Knopf, 1973).

Journey Home, by Yoshiko Uchida (Simon & Schuster, 1978).

Knots in My Yo-Yo String, by Jerry Spinelli (Knopf, 1998).

Let the Circle Be Unbroken, by Mildred D. Taylor (Puffin, 1991).

Living Up the Street, by Gary Soto (Laurel Leaf, 1992).

One Fat Summer, by Robert Lipsyte (HarperCollins, 1991).

Roll of Thunder, Hear My Cry, by Mildred D. Taylor (Dial, 1976).

Starring Sally J. Freedman as Herself, by Judy Blume (Bradbury, 1982).

A Summer Life, by Gary Soto (Laurel Leaf, 1991).

The Little House series, by Laura Ingalls Wilder (HarperCollins, 1994).

Adult Books

These are books that, while intended for an older audience, have high appeal for upper elementary and middle school students. Some of the material in these books may not be appropriate for all age levels, but certainly excerpts from them could be used in the writing workshop classroom.

An American Childhood, by Annie Dillard (HarperCollins, 1988).

Angela's Ashes, by Frank McCourt (Scribner, 1996).

Autobiography, by Benjamin Franklin (NTC Publishing, 1998).

Birds, Beasts and Relatives, by Gerald Durrell (Viking, 1969).*

Black Boy, by Richard Wright (HarperCollins, 1998).

The Classic Slave Narratives, edited by Henry Louis Gates, Jr. (Mentor, 1987).

Coming of Age in Mississippi, by Anne Moody (Laurel Leaf, 1989).

Dandelion Wine, by Ray Bradbury (Random House, 1975).

The Dark Child: An Autobiography of an African Boy, by Camara Laye (Hill and Wang, 1954).*

Dispatches, by Michael Herr (Knopf, 1977).

The Duke of Deception: Memories of My Father, by Geoffrey Wolff
(Vintage, 1990).

Dust Tracks on a Road, by Zora Neale Hurston (Modern Library, 1997).

Growing Up, by Russell Baker (NAL/Dutton, 1992).

The House on Mango Street, by Sandra Cisneros (Random House, 1994).

I Know Why the Caged Bird Sings, by Maya Angelou
(Random House, 1970).

Into Thin Air, by Jon Krakauer (Villard, 1997).

Iron and Silk, by Mark Salzman (Vintage, 1987).

A Leg to Stand On, by Oliver Sacks (Simon & Schuster, 1998).

Life on the Mississippi, by Mark Twain (New American Library, 1997).

Manchild in The Promised Land, by Claude Brown
(Simon & Schuster, 1990).

Maus: A Survivor's Tale, by Art Spiegelman (Vol. 1: Pantheon, 1986; Vol. II:
Pantheon, 1992).

My Family and Other Animals, by Gerald Durrell (Viking, 1977).

Never Cry Wolf, by Farley Mowat (Bantam, 1983).

This Boy's Life, by Tobias Wolff (HarperCollins, 1990).

Two Years Before the Mast, by Richard Henry Dana (Viking, 1981).

Vedi, by Ved Mehta (Norton, 1987).

Walden, by Henry David Thoreau (Vintage, 1998).

The Woman Warrior, by Maxine Hong Kingston (Knopf, 1976).

---

* Indicates books that are out of print.